The Library of
Turtles and Tortoises ™

Spiny Softshell Turtles

Christopher Blomquist

The Rosen Publishing Group's
PowerKids Press ™
New York

For Carolyn, a friend to kith and creatures

Published in 2004 by The Rosen Publishing Group, Inc.
29 East 21st Street, New York, NY 10010

First Edition

Editor: Natashya Wilson
Book Design: Michael J. Caroleo

Photo Credits: Cover and title page © Joe McDonald/Animals Animals; pp. 4, 8, 19 © Bill Beatty; p. 7 © Paul Freed/Animals Animals; p. 11 © G. & K. Illg/Animals Animals; p. 12 © Joe McDonald/CORBIS; p. 15 © J. & F. Burek/Animals Animals; p. 16 © Zig Leszczynski/Animals Animals; p. 20 (top) © Tom Brakefield/CORBIS; p. 20 (bottom) © Alan Schein Photography/CORBIS.

Blomquist, Christopher.
Spiny softshell turtles / Christopher Blomquist.— 1st ed.
     v. cm. — (The library of turtles and tortoises)
Includes bibliographical references and index.
Contents: Soft shell, hard bite — Home wet home — Big girls, smaller boys — Built to swim — Dig in! — Mating and nesting — Growing babies — Awake and asleep — Harms to avoid — Not the perfect pet.
ISBN 0-8239-6737-9 (lib. bdg.)
1. Spiny softshell turtle—Juvenile literature. [1. Spiny softshell turtle. 2. Turtles.] I. Title. II. Series.
QL666.C587 B56 2004
597.92—dc21
                                        2002153727

Manufactured in the United States of America

Contents

Soft Shell, Hard Bite

All turtles have shells, but not all turtle shells are alike. Of the 270 **species**, or kinds, of turtles in the world, most have hard, bony shells. However, some turtles have shells that are soft and leathery. These shells are much flatter than hard shells. The turtle looks as if it is carrying a pancake on its back! Turtles with this type of special shell belong to a group called the softshell turtles.

The spiny softshell turtle is a member of this group. The "spiny" part of its name comes from the tiny spines, or pointy tips, on its shell. The spines on the edge of the shell near the neck are bigger than the spines on top of the shell. The shell feels like sandpaper!

This turtle's shell is soft, but its bite is not. Spiny softshells have strong jaws and sharp claws. They will bite and scratch if picked up.

This spiny softshell turtle's spines can be seen on the rim of the shell, near the turtle's neck, and where light shines on the shell.

5

Home Wet Home

Spiny softshell turtles are **aquatic** animals, which means that they live in the water. As do all the members of the softshell turtle group, spiny softshell turtles live in freshwater, not salt water. They live in rivers and in quiet ponds and lakes with sandy or muddy bottoms. The softshell family does not belong to the group of turtles called tortoises. "Tortoise" is another name for turtles that live only on land and have round, flat-bottomed back feet.

Spiny softshells are North American turtles. They are found in parts of Canada, the United States, and Mexico. They are **solitary** creatures, which means that they usually live alone. Spiny softshells and all turtles belong to a **class** of animals called **reptiles**. Other reptiles include snakes, lizards, and crocodiles.

This spiny softshell is at home in a pond. The turtle's grayish color blends with the pond bottom, helping the turtle to hide.

This map shows where spiny softshell turtles live in North America.

Spiny Softshell Turtle Homes

Carapace

Plastron
(underneath)

Big Girls, Smaller Boys

In the turtle world, spiny softshell turtles are considered to be medium-size. In this species, the females are bigger than the males. An adult female's **carapace**, or top part of the shell, is from 6 ½ to 21 ¼ inches (16.5–54 cm) long. The carapace of the adult male is from 3 ¼ to 8 ½ inches (8.3–21.6 cm) long. The bottom part of the shell, under the turtle's belly, is called the **plastron**.

Six **subspecies** of spiny softshell turtle live in North America. They are the eastern, the western, the Gulf Coast, the pallid, the Guadalupe, and the Texas spiny softshell turtles. They have different shell patterns and colors. Most have green, brown, or tan shells with dark spots on them. Some have black-ringed spots called **ocelli**. These spots look like eyes.

This eastern spiny softshell turtle has dark spots. Spiny softshells also have two dark lines on each side of their head. They can change their shell color slightly over time to match their homes better.

Built to Swim

Spiny softshell turtles are built for their lives in the water. Their light, bendable shells and webbed feet allow the turtles to swim quickly. As do all reptiles, spiny softshell turtles breathe with lungs, not gills. However these turtles rarely have to come all the way up for air. Often they breathe by "**snorkeling**." To snorkel, a softshell turtle stays completely underwater except for its long nose, which it pokes through the water's surface. The turtle snorkels either while floating in the water or when it has buried itself in a river or lake bottom. Spiny softshell turtles can also **absorb** some oxygen directly from the water, through certain areas of skin on their throat and back end. Breathing this way, a spiny softshell turtle can stay underwater for up to 5 hours at a time.

This spiny softshell is snorkeling while buried in a stream bottom. Its nose barely sticks out of the water.

Turtle and Tortoise Facts

Although spiny softshells can stay underwater for five hours, they usually go to the surface to take a breath at least once every 20 minutes when they are moving around.

Dig In!

The long nose of the spiny softshell turtle isn't used just to snorkel. The animal also uses it to sniff out food that's hidden under rocks or among water plants. Spiny softshell turtles are mostly **carnivores**. They enjoy catching and eating aquatic insects, worms, frogs, tadpoles, crawfish, and small fish. They will even eat dead animals. When these turtles do eat plants, it is usually by accident. Pieces of the plant were probably near a tasty piece of meat and got swallowed along with it!

Turtles do not have teeth to chew their food. Instead, they use their powerful, beaklike jaws and sharp claws to tear up their food. The beaklike part of a spiny softshell's jaw is hard to see, because the jaws are covered in fat, fleshy lips. These lips help the turtle to pull food into its mouth.

The fleshy lips of this spiny softshell help the turtle to pull the worm it is eating into its mouth.

Mating and Nesting

Spiny softshell turtles **mate** in the water. Mating usually occurs in late spring in deep water. To **court** a female, a male turtle swims up to her and bumps her with his head. About one month after mating, the female spiny softshell turtle comes ashore. She takes up to 1 hour to dig a nest, usually in a nearby sandbar. The nest she makes is about 4 to 10 inches (10–25 cm) deep. To soften the ground for easier digging, the female may urinate, or release liquid body waste, on the ground. The mother turtle lays from 4 to 30 golf ball–size eggs. The eggs are round with hard shells. She covers them with the sand, then makes her way back to the water. She never returns to the nest. Once her eggs are buried, her job as a parent is done. When the babies hatch, they take care of themselves.

This female Guadalupe softshell may have come onto land to nest. Guadalupe softshells live only in south-central Texas.

Turtle and Tortoise Facts

Most spiny softshell females make two nests per mating season. This helps to ensure that some of the eggs will hatch even if the other eggs are eaten by animals.

Growing Babies

If the eggs aren't uncovered and eaten by animals such as raccoons and skunks, the baby turtles will usually hatch sometime in late August through October. It takes about 60 days for the eggs to hatch. The baby turtles, called **hatchlings**, are about 1 ¼ to 2 inches (3–5 cm) long when they are born. When they dig themselves out of the nest, the first thing they do is head for the water! Spiny softshell hatchlings know how to swim when they are born. All the babies are born with olive or tan shells with spots. The males will keep this look throughout their lives. The shells of the females get patchy as the females get older. Spiny softshells become adults in about 3 to 4 years.

This is a young eastern spiny softshell turtle. Spiny softshell hatchlings have a border of spots on the edge of the shell.

Awake and Asleep

Spiny softshell turtles are **diurnal** animals, which means that they are awake in the daytime. Aside from swimming and hunting, these animals have another favorite daytime activity. They **bask**, or lie in the warm sun, on a rock or a log near the water. Turtles are **cold-blooded** creatures, so basking helps them to warm their bodies. If a spiny softshell turtle senses danger as it basks, it will dive into the water in a split second. These turtles move fast. Some spiny softshells can outrun a human on land! At night these turtles sleep underwater, buried in the sand or the mud. In winter, they **hibernate** underwater, also buried in sand or mud. They stay still and use very little energy. The energy that the turtle does use comes from the fat stored in its body. Hibernating spiny softshells breathe through their skin.

This spiny softshell rests while buried in the mud. This is how the turtle will hibernate through the winter.

Harms to Avoid

Even though spiny softshell turtles can move quickly and can fight back if they are caught, these animals aren't always safe from danger. Hatchlings and young turtles are often **prey** for raccoons, skunks, foxes, snakes, and large fish. Turtles can also get sick if germs get into their shells.

The greatest danger to adult turtles is humans. Most spiny softshell turtles are put at risk by pollution. Buildings put up along rivers and lakes have destroyed many of the turtles' nesting areas. Poisons used to kill unwanted fish have also killed many turtles. Some people even like to eat this species. In certain areas, such as Canada, this species has almost disappeared. There are now laws in place in Canada and in some parts of the United States to protect these turtles and their nesting areas.

Top: *Foxes will eat spiny softshell eggs and babies.*
Bottom: *Pollution from factories such as this oil refinery on a riverbank in North Carolina can make spiny softshells sick.*

Not the Perfect Pet

In April 1979, the Canadian government honored the spiny softshell turtle by putting its picture on a postage stamp. Today people continue to value this special species of turtle. However, these animals do not make good pets. They will hiss, scratch, and bite if they are touched. They also need a lot of special care. Pet spiny softshells need to live in very large fish tanks to stay healthy. The tanks must be able to hold at least 75 gallons (284 l) of water. Expensive pumps are needed to keep the water clean. Spiny softshells must be handled carefully, and only by people who are trained to work with them. If you are lucky enough to see a spiny softshell in the wild, watch it, then leave it alone to enjoy its turtle life of swimming, eating, and basking in the sunshine.

Glossary

absorb (ub-ZORB) To take in and hold on to something.

aquatic (uh-KWAH-tik) Living or growing in water.

bask (BASK) To lie in the sunshine.

carapace (KER-uh-pays) The upper part of a turtle's shell.

carnivores (KAR-nih-vorz) Animals that eat other animals.

class (KLAS) A group of animals with similar traits.

cold-blooded (KOHLD-bluh-did) Having a body heat that changes with the surrounding heat.

court (KORT) To try to gain another's interest.

diurnal (dy-UR-nul) Active during the daytime.

hatchlings (HACH-lingz) Baby animals that have just come out of their eggs.

hibernate (HY-bur-nayt) To spend the winter in a sleeplike state.

mate (MAYT) To join together to make babies.

ocelli (oh-SEH-lee) Spots that look like eyes.

plastron (PLAS-tron) The bottom, flatter part of a turtle's shell that covers the belly.

prey (PRAY) An animal that is hunted by another animal for food.

reptiles (REP-tylz) A group of cold-blooded animals with lungs and scales. Turtles, snakes, and lizards are types of reptiles.

snorkeling (SNORK-ling) Breathing underwater through an air tube.

solitary (SAH-lih-ter-ee) Spending most time alone.

species (SPEE-sheez) A single kind of living thing.

subspecies (SUB-spee-sheez) Types within a species. For example, Siberian tigers and Sumatran tigers are subspecies of tigers. The Siberian tiger's fur is longer and thicker and looks different from the Sumatran tiger's fur.

Index

Web Sites

Due to the changing nature of Internet links, PowerKids Press has
developed an online list of Web sites related to the subject of this book.
This list is updated regularly. Please use this link to access the list:
www.powerkidspress.com/ltt/spiny/